THE
NINETY NINTH
NIGHT

TC FRANKLIN

Sasha,

alignment is necessary.

Always!

Thank you
TC

A pimp. A prostitute. Their abandoned
child. A dream job at The White House,
couldn't fulfill his quest for truth.

A TRUE STORY OF FAITH, HUMILITY
AND DETERMINATION

DEDICATION

I dedicate this book to my mom and dad,
Judy and Frank Calhoun

CONTENTS

CHAPTER ONE

February 24, 2012, was my first day at yet another new job in yet another new city. This time, I found myself in a mega-town, one in which I swore to never live—Los Angeles, California. Each morning thereafter, I awoke to smog-filled skies and miles of bumper-to-bumper traffic. So much for professing the word "never." However, the arduous and history-laden path I chose to arrive at this pivotal date, time, and place, has been deemed by friends and family alike to be more than incredible. The odyssey began out of pure fatigue, coupled with mental, spiritual, and physical exhaustion. I had grown surprisingly weary.

The move west was my rebirth, my road to redemption. It was, in fact, the calling of a frightened spirit in need of awakening. A badly needed change of venue can often do wonders for transformation and enlightenment. New scenery and the need for new people catapulted me from Florida to Denver, Colorado. Why Colorado? Hang tight, there's lots more. Here's where my life's history can help you understand a single man's dilemma with an internal, restless search for my soul's sole purpose.

According to my outrageously bizarre natural parents, whom I met for the first time as a senior in college, I was conceived in the Mile-High State. Many in my small hometown had come to know my birth parents for their wickedly entertaining shenanigans, covering decade after decade: A shouting match here, a gunshot there, and lots of drinking and partying, to say the least.

Elizabeth (aka Roxanne) Scott (more on her alias in a bit) is my birth mother. She has mentioned time and time again that her life had been, for the most part, a nightmare. She crisscrossed the country, attempting repeatedly to escape a horrendous, brain-washing relationship at the hands of my estranged biological father. As if these foiled races to rescue herself weren't bad enough, there was the mental and physical abuse from my hot-tempered natural father, Richard "Dickey" Scott.

Like a cunning chess player, Dickey wouldn't cease until he learned her moves and subsequent whereabouts, tracking her down only to return her to his insane fortress. Elizabeth had learned she was pregnant and needed to vanish in order to bring a child into a very tumultuous world. During what would be her last attempt to escape in December 1961, she had managed to somehow briefly live in Denver. Dickey apparently arrived inside city limits, and upon locating her, pleaded for her to return to the Midwest. The pair eventually drove back, "newly pregnant," to what would become my official birthplace, Springfield, Ohio.

Upon my birth nine months later in September 1962, they raised me for thirty days. Like I said, my natural parents were a bit odd, not stable at all. I was named Jeffery Scott, and after four weeks of playing "family," they abruptly placed me up for adoption. The scenario reminds me of a certain biblical scripture centering on Moses, a scripture I can now relate to. Exodus 1:22: "She placed the baby inside a basket in the tall grass that grew along the banks of the Nile." Apparently Dickey forced Elizabeth to regret giving birth and decide that a brand-new baby, *any* baby, was too much to care for. How awful, you say? An adorable, multiracial baby handed over to authorities at Clark County Children's Home like the return of an ugly birthday sweater! Well, read on, you'll soon learn it was a blessing in disguise for baby Jeff. You see…my biological father was a pimp, my biological mother, his number-one prostitute.

I was adopted five months later on Valentine's Day,

February 14, 1963 and named Timothy F. Calhoun. More on why I chose to take stock in renaming myself later in this book.

The family that nurtured me into who I've become today are, to me, my *real* father and *real* mother, Frank and Judy Calhoun. A tirelessly tenacious workaholic and a man of few words, Frank possessed the courage of a lion, the strength of ten horses, and the entrepreneurial spirit to rival any corporate CEO of modern-day America. Frank is a true die-hard NASCAR oval track race fanatic and without a doubt (at least to me), *the* toughest, smartest guy I know.

My *real* mother, Judy Calhoun, is a saint. Truly, a "saint." A brilliant woman who has given of herself countless years of encouragement, support, motherly love, correction when needed, and always an open, forgiving heart to everyone she has ever met. A retired nurse of forty years, Judy has won countless community awards, including woman of the year at her local church. The Calhoun's raised me on solid principles. Education was always first, playtime later. My mom, deeply faith based, also instilled in me that always telling the truth is the best policy in life and to always say my prayers daily. I took each and every one of my parents' "life lessons" seriously and went on to excel in high school as a student athlete. I graduated college with honors, receiving a degree in journalism from Central State University and studied at the Ohio State University as well. During my years as a White House news correspondent, I was able to give back to my parents. Daytona 500 for Frank on the very year Dale Earnhardt lost his life on the final lap. I brought my mom to Washington, DC, for dinner with President Bill Clinton and Hillary Clinton, inside the West Wing of 1600 Pennsylvania Avenue. The least I could do for the *real* parents who adopted me and gave me the best life anyone could offer, with the love and security I deserved.

I decided to retire from news reporting and chose a more purposeful life in fitness. After returning to school for further education in kinesiology, I became one of the best certified personal trainers in the Tampa Bay area. Sure, it was a 180-degree career move but a career move I realized is more important than being overly worked and overly stressed from endless nights of covering political sensationalism on Capitol Hill. For my soul and the physiques of those to come, health and wellness quickly became top priority.

One of the nicest things about the "Sunshine State" is that it sparked a new beginning and a safe community to raise my son. I tackled that mission solo, having divorced my first wife in March of

1999. My ex-wife also had a son, Ryan, from a previous relationship. I instantly became a step-father to Ryan and raised him the best I could with what I knew at the time. At the time of my divorce, Ryan spent a year with his brother and me in Savannah, Georgia. The brief stint there coincided with a very sad period in all our lives. That transition enabled Ryan to mature enough and move out on his own. Ryan has since settled in Ohio and has two children. I later decided my son, Chad, and I would move to Florida and start anew.

As my training career flourished, my son matured into an outstanding man. He graduated high school and put a few years of college under his belt before deciding to enlist in the US Air Force. Chad is currently living in Chicago, gainfully employed. It's been said that many parents dream of the day they finally experience the proverbial "empty nest."

But after a half a dozen years of personal training, a lengthy relationship with an Eastern European woman that broke off, and a rebound relationship with a Latino woman, which ended badly, the rooms of my home echoed emptiness. My restless soul craved an escape from Florida. Thoughts of relationships gone awry and mixed visions of "where" to go circled my mind.

Not one to ponder too long, I summoned resiliency

and put it to good use. I also recalled quite vividly a few poignant words from my late grandfather: "Hey, there comes a day when it's time to shit or get off the pot." So, I gave away *all* my furniture, packed my car with clothing, a tent, food, an Igloo cooler, bid farewell to close clients and friends, put together a small bundle of cash, and drove 3,000 miles west, in search of a new home.

* * *

"SUCCESS IS TO BE MEASURED NOT SO MUCH BY THE POSITION THAT ONE HAS REACHED IN LIFE AS BY THE OBSTACLES WHICH HE HAS OVERCOME WHILE TRYING TO SUCCEED."

~BOOKER T. WASHINGTON

CHAPTER TWO

The devil is real. He tries each day to disrupt any and all positive spiritual growth in each of us. In fact, I held onto many weaknesses and inner turmoil and had fleeting thoughts of resorting back, even turning around during my road trip and contemplated rejoining a dysfunctional romantic relationship.

This one relationship had its good times, but I've learned when two strong-willed people begin to clash, a breakup is inevitable. I toiled in thought, mile after mile, during my travels west and soon deemed enough was enough. But for whatever reason, my thoughts kept recounting the lesson learned from sinking into seven years of a relationship full of mind games. It was a love interest that truly devastated my heart. But for whatever reason, the good lord, the universe, call it what you will, pulled me away from "Seminole Country." Apparently I needed help in avoiding the need to revisit the risk of continued hurt and emotional upheaval.

Thirty-seven hours and twenty-five minutes due west from Florida, traveling nonstop through six states, I encountered several midsummer rain and dust storms. I arrived midmorning at Ami's Acres Campground at Glenwood Springs, Colorado, 160 miles northwest of Denver. It was here I called an eight-by-eight tent home.

Thanks to a few connections, I found a new place to practice my passion as a personal trainer. The Roaring Fork Club in Basalt, Colorado, is west of Glenwood. I enjoyed fresh-air living at its finest, and living accommodations were pretty cheap. One month of camping, with electric and a bath house was under three hundred bucks.

It was as if the "sleep gods" had delivered the absolute perfect pad. Note to travelers: if you're looking for the best, most peaceful rest, absolute pure, mental and physical R and R, go camping. Not the spoiled RV type of camping but sleeping on the "ground," in my opinion, is simply the best.

Here's where I have to admit, and while you're at it, hold onto your thermals, camping is great and all, restfulness is cool, but camping, forever? This can't last. Can it? Will it? I have to make a real living? I must put a roof over my head? Personal training at Roaring Fork was incredible, the members, trainers, management, and staff were kind beyond measure.

But mountain living is seasonal. If you're fortunate you have four to five months of great weather, the remaining months…well, let's just say, if you don't have a log cabin and a four-by-four truck, you better learn how to build igloos, because high-mountain snowfalls are no joke.

So, a quick decision was mandatory. I made the decision to drive down from the mountain back to civilization. Denver, Colorado, here I come.

* * *

"YOU ARE NEVER TOO OLD TO SET ANOTHER GOAL OR TO DREAM A NEW DREAM."

~C.S. LEWIS

CHAPTER THREE

I called the Cherry Creek Athletic Club in Denver, Colorado, as I drove down the mountain. Cold weather quickly approached. Little did I know that a resume I mailed in a few months earlier was like a well-stocked savings account, there when you need it.

The hiring gods apparently kept vigil over my predicament. As it turned out, the athletic director at Cherry Creek offered me a personal training position on the spot. I quickly found an apartment and settled in. From my window, I looked back up at the mountain, gathering my thoughts about my fascinating yet not-quite-finished journey.

Training is a calling. The best trainers find themselves in exactly the right club, at exactly the right time. It was a burst of energy, a needed spirit inside Cherry Creek Athletic Club that I was summoned to accomplish. Within a few short weeks of prospecting potential clients, I had a packed training schedule for nearly each day of the week. I also taught boot camp and spinning classes at my usual high intensity, and before long, my classes had a waiting list. My God-given talents were shining brightly again. You are "just what this club needs," said upper management, and it gave me a great feeling indeed.

But corporate pay to employees isn't always fair. Until you sign the checks as an owner of your own club, from a trainer's perspective, you're generally at the mercy of the house. The split is generally 65 percent house, 35 percent trainer. Within six to nine months of tireless hustle, you may reach sixty-forty or even fifty-fifty, but those numbers are rare. Trainers often seek work outside of their clubs to make ends meet.

As time wore on, my spirit base grew exponentially. I received a book entitled, *Bible in One Year*, and within my fourth month in Denver, and on January 1, I made a covenant with myself and God to spend time in scripture daily.

I began to see change almost immediately. First, my thinking transformed. Simple thoughts at first, like how can I share a larger amount of positive words? How can I do more for everyone I meet? How can I become more involved in community improvement missions?

So, I jumped at what became my first true experience upon arriving in Denver. It happened in a Starbucks in the suburb of Glendale. While waiting on my café au lait, I noticed an ad seeking mentors. I had been a substitute high school teacher for a couple years while living in Ohio, helping Ryan settle with opportunities of continued education and employment. I called the number on the community post board, hanging high above the condiment rack and eventually interviewed and then joined Byrne Urban Scholars. Their mentoring program for teenagers reaches thousands of Denver area kids, and it's where I was matched and eventually met an incredible family from Mexico.

I was paired with the Hernandez family, Maria, Elberto, and their fourteen-year-old son, Josh. I instantly hit it off with Josh. A great young man, smart, mature beyond his years, and with dreams and goals that I know he will one day reach. I talked with Josh about life, relationships, the business world, college. We went to a variety of venues. We saw movies, played one-on-one and group basketball games, shopped at the mall, but what was a specific thing Josh wanted to experience? He had always wanted to eat at Applebee's, so we went and went and went nearly every weekend for three months during NFL football.

I took a deep liking to Josh and his family, and as the months from October 2011 to January 2012 came and went, I felt as though I was part of their family. They lived in a mobile home community. Josh and his family are the most humble, peaceful, generous people I've met. It was hard to break the news to them that I was considering moving on, especially as I had just arrived a few short months ago to Colorado.

But a restless spirit must move. Stagnation is for me, my enemy. Sitting still is not an option. Within six short months, I was feeling yet another spiritual draw to another locale. As I was getting set to announce my move even further west, I had asked Josh if there was anything his parents needed or wanted. Josh said, his mom and dad were finally getting a house, and they'd never lived in one, only mobile homes, and it would really make him happy if I could somehow buy them a real bed. He went on to say that they had been sleeping on the floor for as long as he could remember. In my soul, I knew I had come to Colorado for more than a training job at Cherry Creek Fitness Club. I had just purchased a brand-new mattress only two months prior to Josh's request. Having barely slept on it, my upcoming move, the mattress, all had its own timing, its own place in God's bigger plan. So, I told Maria and Elberto I was moving to California and would miss them very much but would keep in touch. The very next day, Josh and I carried the mattress down three flights of stairs, and I strapped it to the top of my SUV. While his parents were out running errands, Josh and I quickly moved it into the Hernandez's first-ever new home. Josh and I went out for a bite to eat at his favorite restaurant, and upon returning to his home, we saw that the lights had been turned on. When he and I entered, the look of amazement and humble appreciation covered their faces. Not a word was exchanged yet, we all collectively joined in a moment of silent happiness. I knew I had touched their hearts.

* * *

"ACTIONS PROVE WHO
SOMEONE IS WORDS
PROVE WHO THEY
WANT TO BE."

~UNKNOWN

CHAPTER FOUR

I left Colorado for California February 6, 2012. Six months prior, I had driven from Florida, praying, wondering, what in the world am I doing? The questions I had looming in my mind became much clearer as I drove through Los Angeles and further north up the Pacific Coast Highway toward Santa Barbara. I had met a few people while I was in Denver who had connections to a fitness expert near City College. I checked out a quaint yet private training studio in Summerland, California. The thought of a quiet place to amass a better means of financial stability seemed appealing. I had visions of helping my parents and my sons, and it gave me a goal, a mission, a new adventure.

Santa Barbra is B-E-A-U-T-I-F-U-L, but for whatever reason, I didn't get a pure, authentic feel that I truly belonged there. So, after an ocean-front lunch, I decided to put my energy into dreams of stardom in the "City of Angels," Los Angeles.

"Welcome to Los Angeles" beamed a graffiti-sprayed road sign as I drove south along the 405. An interesting stretch of road, full of aggressive drivers, texting, and weaving, as if not a care in the world. The 405 is definitely not your typical six-lane infrastructure but instead a great place for future NASCAR wannabes to hone driving skills. I knew then and there on that late February afternoon that I would do everything in my power to avoid driving it.

This is where I begin to think and feel my birth parents DNA fully permeated my body. My story is as bizarre as their early actions. TC, adopted shortly after birth, a high school and college track standout, single father, former news anchor/reporter, former high school teacher, personal trainer, moved to LA., with a job waiting, but no place to live, essentially homeless. *Yes*, I *truly* begin my story here.

* * *

CHAPTER FIVE

Ninety-Nine Nights

LAX is located adjacent to the Century City business corridor at Century Boulevard and La Cienega and became the cornerstone of my first three months of existence in Los Angeles. A seemingly odd place to find comfort, but it made sense, at least briefly. I parked inside a small cul-de-sac at La Cienega Boulevard and 9700 South, a spot I would soon know as home.

"Home is where the heart is" is derived from Greece. The translation: "There is no place like home." So, for ninety-nine days and nights, nestled alongside an additional car camper-trailer, I commandeered the backseat of my 2003 Ford Explorer and made it my mobile apartment. Living out of an SUV for ninety-nine nights, at the moment, made practical sense to me.

Call me crazy, bizarre, a man without a plan. But, I must set the tone for how I derived at a decision to sleep in my car. In the middle of February 2012, I didn't anticipate this car-sleeping scenario—not for a single minute in my entire life. Like an infant who doesn't know the iron is hot, or the electric socket will deliver a shock. You don't understand the lesson until you've done the deed. Experience has been historically the best teacher. Now, mind you, I did have somewhat of a plan upon completing a casting call in Denver, and the plan appeared to be on course. I had booked one gig, which would eventually pay quite well. I still had roughly two weeks to get busy and hopefully book more castings through my agency, Wilhelmina, Denver division. I also had secured a new personal training post for Equinox Sports Club in West LA, but the onboarding process didn't begin until February 24, 2012.

So, with time to kill, I drove back and forth, Denver to LA, LA to Denver. I truly began enjoying and accepting my lifelong whirlwind state of mind. It was an attempt to make sense of my "off- the-wall mentality."

For the first time in my life, I truly had to "let go" and let God. My faith wavered sometimes but leaned more toward being strengthened in the spiritual realm. Thanks to my connection with Pastor Gil Jones from Pathways church, I reawakened God's grace and promise. I humbled myself and contacted several clients I had briefly trained with during my short stint at Cherry Creek Athletic Club and asked them if I could stay at their home a night or two...or three. Kindness and life began to unfold as I ran between casting calls while waiting to settle somewhere in LA.

* * *

"GROWTH IS PAINFUL.
CHANGE IS PAINFUL.
BUT NOTHING IS AS
PAINFUL AS STAYING
STUCK SOMEWHERE YOU
DON'T BELONG."

~MANDY HALE

CHAPTER SIX

The two-week lull in my transition bought me back to Colorado and the friendship I developed with Chad and Marci Jenkins. They attended my first spinning class at Cherry Creek Athletic Club. Marci was expecting the couple's first child, but pregnancy didn't stop her even into her third trimester. We hit it off instantly. Both are seasoned triathletes and knew a great workout when they encountered one. Marci was thirty-five weeks pregnant and stormed though each class as fit as anyone not pregnant. Chad also spun and purchased a block of personal training sessions with me, and I helped him truly transform his physique. I, of course, made sure he remained diligent, as I kicked his ass three, sometimes four days a week. When he started his training program, he could barely complete eight pull-ups, which is as much as he could complete in the allotted three-minute time limit. Within three months, Chad could grind out seventeen straight pull-ups. The look on his face upon completion of his new personal best, let's just say it was a "Kodak" moment. Chad, if you're reading this book, you better be able to crank out twenty-five pull-ups by now, like you said you would! By the way, Chad and Marci welcomed into the world a son, and they named him Mixon.

I write their story not out of favorable bias but in all sincerity. With new baby and all that goes with being first-time parents and newlyweds, the Jenkins opened their quaint downstairs guest bedroom to me for an entire ten days during my transition. At the time, they were under the impression that I had everything figured out regarding LA and was just finishing up prearranged print modeling work and had a secure job. And I did, sort of. God puts the right people in front of you at exactly the right time.

Ten days down, two weeks to go until I had to be in Los Angeles. I spent my remaining days in Denver bouncing around to Doz Bog Coffee shops, movie theaters, restaurants, and a few speakeasy bars, saying good-bye to clients and friends I'd met while in Denver. Another client also allowed me to stay rent free for a few days and even took me out to dinner for a belated Christmas gift. Thanks, Lane Waneka; you and Miss Lucy rock!

With my new job start date of February 24 closing in, I had to devise a definitive plan on where to live, and quickly.

Target shopping centers have the best items. Many a time, I'd walk through aisle upon aisle searching for, ah…I don't know, whatever I "thought" I needed. But in your mind, what you need to buy when you realize you'll be living in and out of your car sparks new perspective on simplicity.

You rule out bulky items like furniture, bedside reading lamp, or a coffeemaker, and who needs a shower curtain living in a car?

* * *

"Happiness is not determined by what's happening around you, but rather what's happening inside you."

~ Anonymous

CHAPTER SEVEN

Growing up as a kid back in Ohio, the school year always lasted from September to the end of May, exactly 180 days long. As summer break approached, there was always a class clown or stand-alone rebel rouser and sometimes even our anxious teacher, who used the blackboard as a makeshift calendar, counting down the final days of class. "Eleven days to go…six days to go." Finally, the last day culminated with a huge outdoor party for each grade level. It was customary back then to bring colorful squirt guns and tiny water balloons, fill 'em up at the maintenance shop water facet and dole out endless water blasts of soaked, tie-dyed T-shirt fun. It was within a day or two after you were congratulated by your family and friends on making it to the next grade level, and you couldn't wait to start your ninety days of summer break. Then it was up at dawn, playing outside until the street light came on and still begged your mom for five more minutes of playtime because you didn't dare go in the house when your team was up with a score of six to five in your championship kickball game. If you succumbed to your mom's relentless call to come in for dinner, you faced being called a "chump" for quitting early, and you carried with you the nickname for the entire summer. Meanwhile, Mom always stood vigil at the window, somehow managing to keep the peace and let play continue for an extra five, OK…eight minutes.

Days like those were a time to seek adventure. Another of my favorite pastimes was to build tree houses and outdoor "boys only" tree forts. Looking back, I now know it was God's early design that I needed this rustic, creative spurt to gain knowledge of temporary living quarters. No items were too big, so they wouldn't take up much space in our makeshift command post. My friends and I always had to readjust our walls and roof to keep "spies," usually the girls, from peeking into our clubhouse made from downed tree branches and any of Dad's unused two-by-four lumber scraps he kept strewn throughout the family garage.

Those skills came in handy a mere forty years later. I was in Colorado on a brisk Monday afternoon, having just had my third cup of coffee and cup of oatmeal, which brings me back Target. I knew I needed something to block out the "public" from peering into my car windows. It's amazing what the need for privacy means when you know you're about to be homeless. Construction paper would work great. I remember the numerous art projects I had completed as a student in elementary school, and I knew I could rely on this sturdy, cardboard-like material for my most creative project ever. Easily cut and able to fit any surface area, the makeshift curtain for each of my windows from the inside looking out made for a cozy, darkened interior. I chose white material instead of black because I knew dark would absorb heat from the sun, making the interior quite warm. So, I purchased five, twenty-four by thirty-six-inch sheets of white construction paper for a buck thirty-two each. Curtains for less than ten dollars...priceless!

* * *

"Keep Your thoughts positive because your thoughts become **YOUR WORDS.**

Keep your words positive because your words become **YOUR BEHAVIOR.**

Keep your behavior positive because your behavior becomes **YOUR HABITS.**

Keep your habits positive because your habits become **YOUR VALUES.**

Keep your values positive because your values become **YOUR DESTINY.**"

~Mahatma Gandhi

CHAPTER EIGHT

Leaving Denver was bittersweet. I had arrived only a few months prior, full of new energy and lofty thoughts and goals. I was the new personal trainer in a new city. I had even figured out what church I should attend when I eventually arrived in Los Angeles. Lead pastor Robert Gelinas of Colorado Community Church in Aurora gave me precise direction, as I approached him with details of my relocation and transition. He anointed me with a prayer and said Mosaic church in Hollywood is where I needed to go. Locked in my memory bank, I would soon learn how important his divine intervention would become.

The one thousand-mile journey from Denver heading due west on Interstate 70 was interesting. My former fiancé…yes, the Eastern European gal, the one who I had endured a rocky, six-year, on again, off again relationship! She decided to make an unannounced trip out west and surprised me during my last days in Denver. She boldly claimed our "road to togetherness" began the instant she showed up. I was understandably not as eager to believe her. I did, however, begin to think having company on this leg of my purpose-seeking mission would at least offset the monotony of arduous driving.

Winding roads, mountain elevation and descent, and blizzard-like conditions for two hours of the initial journey, along with "relationship talk," kept us both awake, as the first two hundred miles wore on. I, as most men do, enjoy driving. A leadership role, if you will, driving is the quintessential "freedom mobile" and somehow brings out a bit of macho. Reminiscing about the good times as we listened to memorable music quickly made way for tears, talk, more tears, and then silence. During the simpler days of our relationship, it became commonplace for the two of us to have intellectual discussions, or as I came to know them, mind games. Although I've transformed, I once upon a time would hold on to hurt and disappointment for way too long. It's draining, both physically and mentally. I learned that it's not what the other person necessarily does to you but how you allow it to affect you. I wasn't going to tolerate or listen to her tall tales of eventual broken promises. Or the high probability of her get-bored-quick, rampant infidelity. No, my heart had been mismanaged enough. It's no fun being placed on a backburner, whether it's for a job promotion or not getting picked to play on a team as a kid, it just damages self-esteem. This journey would be the beginning of my road to redemption, and those emotions and that type of life-sucking baggage was being unpacked. Focus was paramount, distractions inadmissible.

I don't want to sound like an old prude, so, let me say more than a few positive things about my former fiancé. She indeed possesses good intention, has a great giving spirit, is smart, funny, and very sexy. But not everyone grows up in a loving household, or for that matter a house filled with any love at all, as was her case. Very cold and opportunistic Eastern European parents with a closed mind regarding a host of worldly subjects, especially interracial dating, made our relationship extremely challenging. Their thought process stood at the forefront and as a roadblock toward what could have been a great thing between us both. But for the most part, she allowed our intimate union to be a secret from her parents for fear they would "disown her," as she put it. While she grew to be extremely intelligent scholastically, in my opinion, there was no common sense taught at home on how to treat people, and in particular, people of color.

As we drove into Los Angeles entering west to east, then south on the 405, I knew it would be only a few days more when this phase of the journey, in every sense, would end.

We both milled around Santa Monica, downtown Los Angeles, even ventured into Hollywood and passed time at restaurants and coffee shops for roughly four days. We managed to spend our less-than-romantic and non-intimate nights at a bed-and-breakfast home we had rented. My attraction toward her felt extremely diminished, and hers to me, I deemed, was more pretend than true and lacked authenticity. It simply boiled down to a "been there, done that" mind-set, and her lingering mannerisms of opportunism and pitiful rescue spoke loud and clear. One more day, I thought, and I'd drop her off at LAX.

The morning of her departure seemed empty. Breakfast, mundane suitcase packing, quick and effortless. The drive to the airport flowed rather smoothly. Once the car stopped, I stepped out instinctively quick, as though a movie set director had shouted, "Action." With a momentous good-bye looming, this particular final farewell appeared to hold no conviction. Her tears, many of which I witnessed before, were to me, simply a display. Warm and fuzzy feelings no more. Our quick hug good-bye was for me more "Hollywood" than, "Hold me tight, dear." It prompted me to move rapidly back toward my door. I drove off and made no motion to look in the rearview mirror. Onward, upward, forward were my thoughts. Where to go and where to stay remained puzzling to me. This chapter of my life came to an end, and yet a new one simultaneously began.

* * *

"NEVER MAKE SOMEONE A PRIORITY WHEN ALL YOU ARE TO THEM IS AN OPTION."

~MAYA ANGELOU

CHAPTER NINE

The first night of the rest of my life began with abundant courage. Dusk had begun to settle on the horizon in Century City, the LA weather…ideal. I drove approximately five miles and thought, "Now what?"

With little clothing, a few blankets, and enough nonperishable food and water for at least one week neatly packed in my car, I decided for the first night to park inside LAX at parking lot *C*. Upon scouring multiple locations, searching for the optimum parking spot, I noticed a rather large road sign that read: *$12.00 dollars per night, overnight parking*.

Life moves fast. No, really fast! Every human being experiences peaks and valleys. Some people make wrong choices, others adopt bad habits and hang onto them throughout life. If you let the tough moments deflate your spirit, diminish your will to succeed, challenges can break you. But they can also *make you*. I decided to reinvent myself with a new name, one I chose. I was given Jeff Scott by my birth parents. I was, for forty-nine years, known as Tim Calhoun. But I decided I wanted to give myself a name of my own. Designed and created by me for me. I decided to use what I thought worked for me. After completing all necessary documents in the LA County Superior Court, the Social Security Administration and all licenses, passport documents and the like, from here on out, I became legally known as TC Franklin.

I embarked on this phase of my life with no real plan. In fact, I've come to know that planning for most Virgos, including myself, doesn't really exist. We are doers. Our qualities are to nurture, care for, or "rescue" others. Yes we are perfectionists, sometimes to a fault. Critical of ourselves beyond measure, we are often our own worst enemies, getting in our own way. My humility, my faith, and my determination played a pivotal role the very night I chose to park my car and sleep in it. It all boiled down to an enormously intense and life-changing, ninety-nine-night odyssey.

* * *

CHAPTER TEN

Climbing between the driver's seat and passenger seat, over the console, and into the back of an SUV takes a little getting used to. Having accomplished this very maneuver with cars I've owned in the past didn't hold much relevance, as it would this particular night. Before I only had to call upon a quick dose of youthful strength and flexibility to jump in the backseat with my high school girlfriend. This night, February 24, 2012, tested my aging body. At exactly six feet tall and fifty years old, I rediscovered what "full range of motion" means. My balance and movement complexities had changed over the years, but I managed to finagle my arms, legs, and torso and crawl cat-like into my compact living quarters. The space was manageable yet snug. The room measured 81.7 cubic feet of living space, these numbers courtesy of my Ford Explorer owner's manual.

The exact length of my makeshift room fit me to a tee. From the edge of the back of the armrest console, where my feet would slightly touch, to the rear hatch door was miraculously a smidge longer than my full, extended body. The width of the interior was four feet. I had brought along several pillows, and when arranged at the rear deck lid, I had a cot-length span to lie down in a coffin-like position and sleep. Directly alongside my shoulders were two suitcases stacked one atop the other.

* * *

CHAPTER ELEVEN

The first night at the airport was not as noisy as one might think. Either I was too exhausted to hear, or on this particular night, LAX just didn't seem so busy with take offs and landings. The night air was an ideal fifty-five degrees. In my favorite pajamas, and with socks on my feet, I said my prayers and decided to lay flat on my back and stare at the interior roof, eighteen inches from my nose. As I drifted off to sleep, a very familiar yet dormant thought raced through my mind. I couldn't help and recalled how thrilled I was to climb to the top of my bunk bed when I was a kid! The feeling of being that close to the ceiling of my bedroom seemed so cool at seven years old. In a sense, it seemed "way cool" at fifty years old to relive that childhood memory.

The next morning, my cell phone alarm clock blared louder than any alarm I've ever heard. The time was four forty-five. It could have been the acoustics inside my car, or I was extremely sound asleep and simply startled awake. I quickly sprung upward, as though I was missing a major event. In an instant, my eagerness met head on with the ceiling. No damage, but I did let out a slight chuckle during the abrupt head-banging collision. I slept so solidly, I momentarily forgot I was in my car. The smile from my mishap remained on my face as I maneuvered my freshly rested body into the front seat. I wiggled into my newly purchased workout gear. New shoes on, I grabbed the matching hat I had placed on my gearshift knob, I thanked God for yet another new day, and cranked up the engine. Having set aside exactly twelve dollars in my armrest, I paid the parking lot attendant and searched for the nearest bathroom. Within a few minutes, I saw the "golden arches" at McDonald's on Century Boulevard. It would quickly become my morning stop for a great cup of coffee for the next three months.

* * *

CHAPTER TWELVE

After a quick refresher, I was off to begin my first day of my new personal training position at Equinox Sports Club. Equinox is a high-end fitness center catering to the affluent and celebrities. Headquartered in New York City, there are over sixty clubs throughout the United States, Canada, and Europe, and it was growing rapidly. In California, there are sixteen clubs. The new franchise club on Sepulveda Boulevard in West Hollywood was formerly the antiquated Sports Club LA before a takeover acquisition by Equinox in late 2011. I was eager to begin my first day alongside nearly a dozen bright-eyed and talented trainers who would begin as "fired up" as I was. With so much to absorb, there wasn't time to fuss over corporate onboarding and policy and procedure details. It was about digging in and doing so diligently. Each new hire anticipated a calendar full of new clients.

My initial thoughts about Equinox had been open-minded. My decade-plus training experience and the confidence to prospect new clients felt like a good fit, as I listened to personal training manager, Mike Martin, welcome our new group. The first day was indeed lengthy, full of note-taking, paperwork, and a tour of the gym's one hundred thirty thousand-square-foot layout. Three stories tall, it covered an entire city block. All new employees are required to "work the floor shift" as many as five times a week during their learning-curve month. Floor shifts can extend for several months until sales "numbers" are met. Once you hit ninety-five one-hour training sessions per month, a new trainer gets the relief of clean-up duty and miles of walking the floor, all in an attempt to be noticed.

I was determined to get as close to, if not surpass the goal within the first full month. After the first ten-hour day came to a close, I knew I had my work cut out for me in many ways. I lingered briefly near the upscale locker room, commencing in idle chit chat with several new colleagues and announced I was heading home for the night. When asked where I was living, I said, "Staying with friends." However, I was driving back to the cul-de-sac at Century City to sleep in my car for the second night.

* * *

CHAPTER THIRTEEN

The late-evening drive wasn't a bother. I managed to go against the grain of crazed motorists on the 405 and took the parallel road, void of bumper-to-bumper madness. I timed my arrival to coincide with nightfall. It was camouflage for overnight parking.

The new and soon-to-be choreographed shuffle of putting on pajamas and crawling into the back seat for some sleep was soon effortless. Before that process began, I got out of the car to relieve myself in the most convenient way known to man. I did so uniquely, hidden behind my partially opened back passenger side door and urinated onto a narrow stretch of grass between the curb and street to avoid being seen by motorists.

I was not the only wayward person living in a mobile unit. There was another occupant at this first-come, first-serve parking area, approximately fifty feet away. He called himself Rodney. He drove a tattered, old Ford pick-up with a hardtop camper attached in the bed. Mostly to himself and very quiet, he owned a mixed-breed dog. He said hello each night as he walked Rosco directly past my car.

My cell phone beamed 10:18 p.m. I set the alarm for 4:45 a.m. I wanted to be first at the gym and begin my next day full of zeal in an effort to meet as many people as possible.

At 3:34 a.m., I was wide awake and raring to go. I thanked Jesus for a decent night's sleep. I quickly kicked off my blanket, removed my socks and PJs, and returned to the front seat. The temperature was a brisk fifty degrees. I didn't mind, as I always endured chilly nights in Ohio. My dad was the king of the thermostat, often keeping the family just above freezing to save money.

Off to work I drove. Finding parking in LA is tricky. "Read the signs," warned each person I encountered when I searched for a space. "No parking between 10:00 p.m. and 5:00 a.m.," read one sign. Another sign warned, "Two-hour parking only, between 8:00 a.m. and 6:00 p.m." Paid parking meters can be your friend and your worst enemy, especially if you forget to pay every two hours while running errands or in and out an office building. I did find parking for up to sixteen hours. After my customary morning phone chat with my mom back in Ohio, which I hadn't missed in over two years, I stepped out of my car and strolled off to learn the ropes at Equinox. It wasn't long before my own extreme workout regimen was noticed by coworkers and regular gym attendees.

* * *

You are **INTENSE**

You are **OBSESSED**

You are **NOT NORMAL**

You say **YES** when other say no

You **RISE** while others sleep

You are **BETTER** today than you were yesterday

You **DO** what others will not

You **CONTROL** your destiny.

You are on a quest

NEVER STOP

~Unknown

CHAPTER FOURTEEN

A ballistic series of upside-down sit-ups is the best for abs, period! Hanging by my ankles and carefully positioned between the hand grips of the pull-up bar, I became a main attraction. Once aloft, I could crank out sets of twenty-five in a row. Forget the outdated six-pack abs, I had developed eight-pack abs of steel. Adding to my workout, I would complete one hundred push-ups, three sets of overhead shoulder press, dumbbell curls, additional sit-ups, and a variety of bodyweight exercises. I dropped ten pounds in the first month and whittled down to 5 percent body fat. I did add seven pounds of lean muscle mass and became the fittest I've ever been.

I also finished each workout with a series of thirty seconds off, thirty seconds on sprint intervals on the treadmill at speeds in excess of twelve and thirteen miles per hour, lasting for thirty to forty-five minutes.

Fit body, fit mind, fit soul. Healthy food has never been so vital. I would eat perhaps the most strict nutritional food items ever in my life. Coupled with being short on cash and the desire to succeed gives the word "hunger" a whole new meaning. I have always been scared of failure, and this time was no different. I wanted to make my own way, and hard work was the remedy.

Hard work pays off. It's not cliché, it is very true. My first client entered the picture within the first week of exhausting prospecting, walking the three-level gym floor for up to fourteen hours each day. I've always been fond of giving people nicknames. Keeping true to my word and refraining from using this particular client's real name, I called her, Sparkles. A fiery redhead, loads of fun, and a potty mouth to boot, Sparkles is a true California-born woman. Raised in the "Valley," she is a notably successful real estate agent. Sparkles's smile can light up any room, and she has spunk. She insisted on the usual request by most, if not all female clients, to tone the butt and build firm muscle in the arms. From day one, we hit it off, and an authentic friendship was formed. Sparkles bought ninety-six one-hour sessions. Incredible for a new trainer in a new town, but like I told her, as I do all my clients, if you want to be the best, you have to train with the best. She would become an even better friend on the ninety-ninth night of my journey. More details on Sparkles later.

As nighttime approached during that last week in February, and fitness assessments and complimentary personal training sessions began multiplying on my calendar, it came time to rearrange my thought process about the end of the workday. I made it my mantra to stay at the club each day from five in the morning to eight thirty at night. Most people who churn out ten to fifteen-hour days perhaps take for granted the fact that they can simply jump in their car and make the routine journey home after a full day at the office. I, on the other hand, temporarily had no physical address, let alone any particular place to be or go. Ralphs grocery store became my nightly ritual. It was here I could get a hot bowl of soup, a fresh piece of cooked salmon, and a block of ice for my cooler to keep my food from spoiling. One employee and I became well acquainted and always spoke more about family and relationships than, "Hello, may I help you?" Her name is Bobbi, a very kind, southern-born, African American woman who has worked for Ralphs for twenty-three years. We saw each other for nearly each of my first ninety-nine nights in LA. As time went on, Bobbi would always greet me with a smile and say, "Let me guess, fish?" I would nod. We began placing a wager as to who could guess the actual weight of each single piece of salmon I would buy. It became so fun that we bet whomever came closest to the price and was first to win ten weigh-ins in a row, the other had to buy a piece of salmon. It took about one month to declare a winner. Let's just say, Bobbi, where is my free fish? I won fair and square: TC = ten, Bobbi = seven.

She claims it was one of my modeling photos that caused her to lose focus. I did have my shirt off in one photo I had taken and given to her.

The nights didn't hinder me from being as comfortable as possible. A makeshift curtain acted as a barrier to what was behind the driver and passenger seats. *Behind the Brown Blanket* was on the list of what to title my book, but *The Ninety-Ninth Night* fit best. My cooler rested perfectly behind the passenger seat and kept a block of ice mostly solid for up to three days. I vividly remember my grandparents using a block of ice to keep their icebox cold. Call me old school, but it worked and worked well. The front seat floor board became my pantry. Almonds, oatmeal, cereal, bananas, and oranges. A disposable twenty-four-count plastic bowl set came to rest behind my center console. Plastic cutlery rested in the pocket of my

driver's side door, along with my daily reader, *The Bible in One Year*.

My sturdy folding table turned bed platform rested flush against the back of the driver's seat. It was layered in mattress pads with twice-folded quilts and several comforters, and that made things comfy. I had propped my bed with foam lifters to counterbalance the tilt of the parked car. I would not neglect to say my prayers. I often managed to crouch to my knees in a yoga child's pose, letting God know I was thankful for yet another day of health and protection. I truly believe he heard every word and gave me a sense of peace like I never knew before. Funny how homelessness humbled me, but I felt more alive, aware, and awake than ever.

* * *

"MAYBE THE JOURNEY ISN'T SO MUCH ABOUT BECOME ANYTHING. MAYBE IT'S ABOUT UN-BECOMING EVERYTHING THAT ISN'T REALLY YOU SO YOU CAN BE WHO WERE YOU MEANT TO BE IN THE FIRST PLACE."

~UNKNOWN

CHAPTER FIFTEEN

Up and at 'em, thanks to my trusty cell phone alarm, and I was eager for the free educational classes offered to new trainers. It would come in handy as I began to train professional Athletes. One professional athlete in particular needed to quickly get back to work with an NFL team. Born and raised in Southern California, Kai Forbath graduated from UCLA in 2009. Kai was one of the NCAA's top place-kickers. His pure talent, mixed with determination, Kai signed with the Dallas Cowboys. Although marred by injuries in college, Kai seemed to be ready for his first NFL preseason in 2011. But as fate would have it, injuries don't always heal properly, and during his first preseason game, Kai reinjured his groin. Crucial to any athlete, the adductor muscle endures a heavy load of force and power. In Kai's case, a severe strain nearly ended his young career. Having never met Kai, another trainer at the club who attended UCLA with Kai introduced us to one another. He informed Kai of one of my specialties, PNF stretching.

Proprioceptive Neuromuscular Facilitation—
agonist/antagonist movement or stretching of
muscle. I offered a free session to Kai and reassured
him that within six weeks, plus core work and PNF,
he'd be better than new. I landed a great client and
an awesome friend. Kai and I went on to see his
range of motion increase by over 60 percent to an
active stretch measurement of his foot, reaching
eight inches over his head. To put in perspective
how well my technique worked, during Kai's first
week of stretch sessions, he couldn't bring his leg
parallel to his waist. Although Dallas traded Kai, he
resigned with the Tampa Bay Buccaneers for the
2012 season and is currently with the Washington
Redskins. As the remaining day wound down at the
club, a few more inquiries were being made about
me—"Who's the new guy?"

Even though I always had a smile on my face, no
one knew how I was living. After another fourteen-
hour-day and a long shower at the club, I headed to
my mobile apartment, and then drove eleven miles
to my parking spot. I didn't dare tell anyone. That
is, until I met my next client.

* * *

CHAPTER SIXTEEN

Nicknamed Drano back when he was in high school in the mid-1980s, this particular client is by far the most fascinating person I've ever met. Don't get me wrong, I've met famous people—Oprah, Bill and Hillary Clinton, Henry Winkler, dozens of professional athletes—but the man called Drano topped them all.

During my third week of training new clients and finding time to work out for myself, I took a quick break and sat down at a company computer to update my calendar. Out of the blue, I heard a voice. "Yo, my man. I been watching you for a week and a half, and we need to train." I looked up and saw a rather large human hovering over me. He was cocky and had an edginess about him. I responded with a quick, "OK!" He turned and walked to the front desk of the club, and I followed quickly behind, not knowing what to expect. He reached into his pocket and pulled out a large wad of cash and said, "How many sessions can I buy with this trainer?" A front desk assistant named Mickey replied, "Well, forty-eight sessions is the max, and it costs about four thousand dollars." Drano began snapping one hundred-dollar bills between his fingers and thumb like a Vegas blackjack dealer. I smiled ever so big on that Thursday afternoon as I signed my second client to forty-eight sessions of personal training. Drano and I decided not to waste any time our first session, the very next morning, which was Friday at eight in the morning.

I quickly received a high five from Mike, my PT manager, and I strolled off to the locker room to grab my car keys and go out to my car and have lunch. My midday snack included a bowl of Cheerios, a can of tuna, a banana, and a few almonds. Healthy is actually cheaper than one might think. I, of course, had mapped out my eating plan well in advance so as not to spend money frivolously each day. Back from lunch, it was time for my evening prospecting to try and drum up more clients. Not every night at the gym is packed. This is LA, and people have plenty to do, and I would soon learn for myself how and where to venture throughout "Tinseltown" to see where I fit among so many fascinating people.

As I woke in my mobile unit once again, my mind was focused on the first programmed training session I would have with Drano.

The first session was progressing smoothly, and I soon learned much more about my newest client. He was deconditioned but carried with him the strength level of a linebacker. Drano made it successfully through the entire hour. He suggested I go out to lunch with him, and since I had a break between clients, I accepted.

Drano and I jumped in his car and drove off. After weaving through traffic, Drano asked me, "So, who is TC? Really, my man, who the hell is TC?" I paused briefly and began giving him the abbreviated version of my life. I informed him of my upbringing, college career, and fifteen-year marriage. He listened intently as I continued with the story of my transformation from out-of-shape news anchor and single father to a super-fit personal trainer. Now in LA, I had come to the West Coast for a change and to try my hand at acting, modeling, and celebrity training. After hearing what I'm sure he thought was a crock, he asked where I was staying, which part of town I was living in.

The moment of truth rang loud and clear in my mind. I said to him after careful deliberation, "Drano, man, I'm living in my car." He looked in awe and snapped back, "What!? Why didn't you tell me when we met? TC, I can't have you living like that, especially a black man I know is trying to make it."

I replied with some hesitation, saying it was a pride thing, that I needed a little humility. "I can change it, Drano, I'm just grinding along, knowing it's going be all right, because God's got me covered."

The silence then became almost surreal, and Drano stared at me and said, "Hold on, man; we gotta make a stop." We then pulled into a luxury high-rise condominium complex and drove to the underground parking garage. Drano told me to hold tight. He sprung from his car and darted off toward an elevator. I sat patiently with the engine running and within ten minutes, he returned.

As he opened his door, he tossed a clump of what seemed like bar of soap in my direction. It landed in my lap, and to my surprise, I glimpsed down at a wad of cash wrapped in a rubber band. I looked in amazement and asked, "What is this—" He cut me off and said. "TC, this ain't no loan, it's a gift! Take it, and get you a spot to rest your head, get your mind and body some peace. You need an apartment, and this should be enough for first and last month's rent."

I was stunned. Not only at his generosity but of his willingness to believe in me when not knowing much about me. I look back now and know it was the hand of God touching Drano's heart and filling my life with a blessing.

I thanked Drano profusely and continue to to this day. We smiled at each other like brothers and drove back to the club. I stepped out of the car with a new sense of purpose and a pep in my step, somehow knowing that things were looking up as I danced along on my amazing journey.

* * *

"I AM HOMESICK FOR A PLACE I AM NOT SURE EVEN EXISTS. ONE WHERE MY HEART IS FULL. AND MY SOUL IS UNDERSTOOD."

~UNKNOWN

CHAPTER SEVENTEEN

Another long day over and a drive back to my parking spot, I changed into my PJs and chatted by phone with my longtime friend Sheila, who resides in Chicago. We caught up on our lives and the many people in them. I then proceeded to share with her my living arrangements. She literally yelled at me in disbelief. Then she said, "I'm amazed you sound so good and peaceful." I said, "Girl, you have no idea; it's the most peaceful I've been in decades." She added how proud she was of my decision to make drastic changes in my life but more importantly that I was beginning to emulate more wisdom in my words and from my heart than in the thirty-two years of knowing one another.

Blessing comes in droves sometimes, and in my instance, it flowed steadily. My next encounter with beneficial people took place with a previously mentioned client—Sparkles.

During one of our training sessions and having known about her real estate career, I asked if she knew of anyone who might have a place to rent and to share that info with me ASAP.

In a split second, she verbalized what instantly became a saving grace kind of moment for me. Sparkles said, "Hey, I have a cottage-style guesthouse behind my home, and the current short-term tenants will be leaving in about three weeks. You can check it out if you want?" I was floored and happy. I said, "Absolutely! I can stop by when it's convenient for you." Within a one-week span, I suddenly went from homeless to hopeful, humbled to happy, as I sat back and thought joyfully of the two new friends entering my life and an awesome blessing from above.

* * *

CHAPTER EIGHTEEN

May 31, 2012, was the first night in my rented guesthouse cottage and was pure bliss. The joy of unpacking my small suitcase with what little clothing it held was actually fun. Walking even felt new. From cramped quarters of an SUV, any movement in any direction felt like a stroll in a park. Although the cottage was small, compared to an actual full-size home, it had all the necessary creature comforts one might expect. A fully dressed king-size bed, two separate sitting areas, with a small flat screen TV. The breakfast nook had the most darling mini table with two standard chairs neatly tucked beneath the table's edge. Midroom, a college-dorm-size fridge and microwave made for a cute, simplistic kitchenette. The bathroom was picture perfect with painted artwork of ocean views hanging on the walls. The tub/shower combo was ideal. I couldn't have felt better after realizing the extent of my blessings. A new job, a few new friends, and the hope of the mystifying unknown that often accompanies any major change of location. With my heart and soul set on making Los Angeles my permanent residence, I felt deep within that when opportunity knocked, I would be ready. For what, I still hadn't figured out yet.

* * *

CHAPTER NINETEEN

Entering June and on into late July, I was robotic, on a machine-like mission to meet and exceed the necessary sales numbers as a personal trainer. Within a few short weeks, I was the number one new hire trainer with over seventy training sessions for an entire month. A smile on my face and eyes seeking new clients at a moment's notice, I would use any downtime to work out the only way I knew how, with extremely high intensity. That intensity apparently didn't go unnoticed. Watchful eyes had been focused on me by regular gym buffs, and as is often the case in LA, they really pay attention to the hottest, latest, most trendy thing. In this case, it was me. Clients began approaching me saying, "I've never seen some of the exercises you do. Do you have a card? Others would complement me on my inversion sit-ups or my outrageous interval treadmill routines. A few clients offered me higher-paying opportunities to train them outside of the club, which became ever so enticing.

One such night, having finished training a client and midway through that client's stretch session, I was caught in a magnificent staring contest. OK, not actually a contest but a look that captured my attention like never before. My eyes locked with a pair of blue eyes from this particular woman, and I had no idea at the time that that "look" would eventually change my life forever. She whisked past the stretch table I was working with my client on and within seconds strolled off around a corner. My client said, "Dude, did you see her look at you?" I was shell-shocked! Me, a guy never at a loss for words, speechless. A couple weeks had gone by since that "look," and due to my busy schedule, I had simply chalked-up the incident as a passing moment. Maintaining focus was still paramount. God works in mysterious ways. I found this out again in a split second. As I sat for a brief spell on a bench between the cardio room and the yoga studio, I texted my next client, confirming our appointment for later that day. Suddenly, a business card was thrust into my face, covering my cell phone. I looked at the card, then glanced up to see who the outstretched arm belonged to. It was the woman I locked eyes with a few weeks ago. She quickly asked me if I had ever tried an aerial workout and if I would like to attend one of her classes. Stunned, I mumbled, "Sure!" She quickly informed me that she was an aerial artist and was instructing class at her loft. She smiled continuously and said I was invited to her next class, which was in two days. I said I would try and make it, and our conversation ended.

I thought for a few hours about our exchange, and over the next day and a half, I pondered going to her class. Having learned that without network there is no net worth, I chose to give my social circle a badly needed boost and went.

* * *

"YOUR FLAWS ARE
PERFECT FOR THE
HEART THAT IS MEANT
TO LOVE YOU."

~TRENT SHELTON

CHAPTER TWENTY

Upon arriving, I had no idea what to expect. I found parking near what looked like an abandoned warehouse and walked cautiously toward a makeshift sign attached to a rusty fence post. The sign read: *Aerial Class 7:00 p.m.* I entered to the sound of great music and several women twirling upside down and right-side up again. They each seemed to do so effortlessly, tethered to beautiful multicolored silk fabric, stretching twenty feet long from ceiling to floor. Upon watching in awe as the instructor assisted her students to move like swans in midair, I was encouraged to give it a try and was told by the lovely and fit instructor that it was more about grace and finesse than brute strength.

Jill was the instructor. I had nearly forgotten her name until I heard one of her clients ask her a question. Jill gave me a brief demonstration on how to hold the fabric between foot and forearm and with a few inchworm pull-ups, I was ten feet off the ground, as though I were floating.

A few giggles came from her clients, as they watched in amazement how I, the only guy in class, was giving it my best effort. I tried looking graceful, but it was full of rough and shaky moves.

As class ended, and Jill's clients left for the evening, I stayed back for a bit to ask her a few questions. Upon returning from showing her clients to their cars, we sat and began to talk about, well, *everything*. And I do mean everything.

For the next four hours, we shared life, the peaks, valleys, fun, and ferociousness of hectic living in big cities and the agonizing issues with former intimate relationships. It's as if we were on the same page, story after story. She shared the very loft she taught in and what I later learned, lived in, with a boyfriend/business partner. He had recently gone back home to Bulgaria. I talked about a former girlfriend I had lived with for six years who was also from Bulgaria. Wow! Having been through anything with anybody from that part of Eastern Europe is a challenge. But for two people who had just met, to have lived through similar relationship issues from Eastern European relations, was rare, if unheard of.

We agreed to laugh it off and call it a night, though we did so reluctantly. A quick hug good-bye, and I walked to my car. She stood at the fence post gate

as I drove off. Seeing her again was on my mind,
and I hoped that seeing me again was on hers, too.

* * *

"THE MEANING OF LIFE
IS TO FIND YOUR GIFT.
THE PURPOSE OF LIFE
IS TO GIVE IT AWAY."

~PABLO PICASSO

CHAPTER TWENTY ONE

The days began to make more sense. For the next several months of 2013 and into 2014, I woke each morning thankful and with sincere purpose. A natural flow to the order of life seemed more meaningful, as I helped people get their bodies in outstanding physical shape by being the best personal trainer I could be.

Jill and I began dating, and we agreed to travel together to her hometown of Sacramento for one of her best friend's weddings. As she and I attended that wedding ceremony, I looked back at how far I had come.

When faith, determination, and humility come together with the human spirit, dreams and truthful thoughts blend harmoniously.

Couple that with proper rest, healthy eating, and exercise, and your inner spirit can resonate energy into reality.

Experience is the best teacher when it comes to gaining wisdom. I've learned quite a bit over the years, perhaps none as important as having "belief" in yourself, no matter your circumstances.

By the way, after finally deciding to finish writing this book a year after I began, I also asked Jill to marry me. We exchanged our own wedding vows, full of happy tears, at a quaint hotel nestled in the heart of Manhattan Beach, California. It was an intimate "family only" ceremony on September 14, 2013.

So far, my journey and the stories amassed cover a mere fifty years. I believe deep in my soul that I'm destined to reach one hundred years of life on earth and I am eager to experience more truth-telling encounters.

I'm looking forward to life with my new bride, and I'm certain to exude more tenacity than ever, meeting each and every minute with fearlessness, authenticity, and a smile.

* * *

Acknowledgments

My parents Judy & Frank Calhoun. If not for your love and guidance, I wouldn't be the man I am today.

My son Chad Calhoun, my step son Ryan James, I LOVE YOU BOTH. Leigh Anne Richardson, THANK YOU for our amazing son and the many memories.

Frankie Jay Robinson, LaShaun V. Spencer, Oscar T. Robinson, Robert Edwards Jr., Fred Brooks, Okay & Emeka Ubah, Rich Stilwell, Coach Earl Taylor, Rey Harris, Anthony Fisher, Tania Zee, Paul and Shay Weinberg, Bill Duke, Chip Johnson, Todd Jackson, Ben Rizzo, The Douthy's. Each and every one of you are indeed the example of what true friends are all about.

Sheila White- You are my saving grace, my friend and confidante. I LOVE YOU dearly.

Chris Johnson-something double, something big. Keep that camera rolling. Love you like a son.

My Harley Davidson wingman- Rich Hansen.

Frank & Lynelle Loriaux- your hospitality is always appreciated.

Connie & Elvin Spreng- I'm coming to visit, I promise.

Carla & Drew Webb- always the best coffee.

Cynthia Baker-Best Bureau Chief-News Director EVER. Thanks for the education in Washington D.C.

AND LASTLY

My wife Jill. The 'LOOK' said it all that fateful day.
Thank you for our bubble and the us-ness of US. You
are forever my 'inside out sock buddy.'

I LOVE YOU UNCONDITIONALLY

ABOUT THE AUTHOR

TC Franklin hails from Springfield, Ohio and received his B.A.in Journalism in the mid- eighties. TC rose to prominence from his first job as a tour guide for CNN, in Atlanta, Ga., to landed his first on-air TV job, as general assignment news reporter in Chattanooga Tennessee.

Within six years TC, powered his way through several major TV news markets including Philadelphia, Denver, Chicago, Miami and New York. He eventually brokered a four year contract with Tribune Broadcasting. His daily regimen included over twenty TV News 'LIVE SHOTS' daily from The White House in Washington D.C. During the Clinton Administration, TC became an Emmy Nominated Journalist who also covered the Supreme Court and Capitol Hill, six days a week.

Upon moving to L.A., TC kept a promise to himself and finally stared in a feature film. A fitness expert and nonfiction writer at heart, TC is now sole owner of a production company, Blue Ribbon Productions, based in Los Angeles. TC's mission in life is to remain diligent in his pursuit of excellence, be it story-telling or directing and casting actors for his numerous stage, TV and film productions. Oh yeah, he loves his wife, Jill, who lets him enjoy riding his Harley Davidson motorcycles and classic VW beetles.

To learn more about TC Franklin please visit:

www.tcfranklin.com

www.blueribbonproductions.com

34594281R00051

Made in the USA
Charleston, SC
13 October 2014